Pillar Press

www.pillarpress.co.uk

2024

What's that Song?

Introduction
Say what you see!

Pictorial brainteasers for those who
want to test their knowledge of
popular songs.
Can you decipher the cryptic clues in
this compilation of
back-of-the-envelope illustration.
The answers can be found at the back
of the book.
Don't be tempted to look too soon.
Give it your best shot!

Songs 1 & 2

Songs 3 & 4

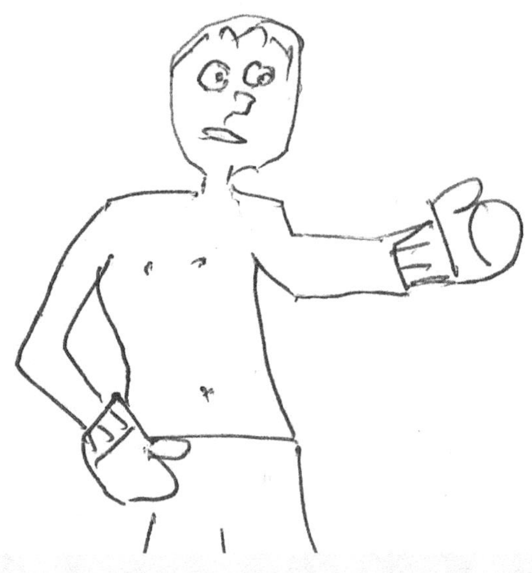

Songs 5 & 6

Songs 7 & 8

Songs 9 & 10

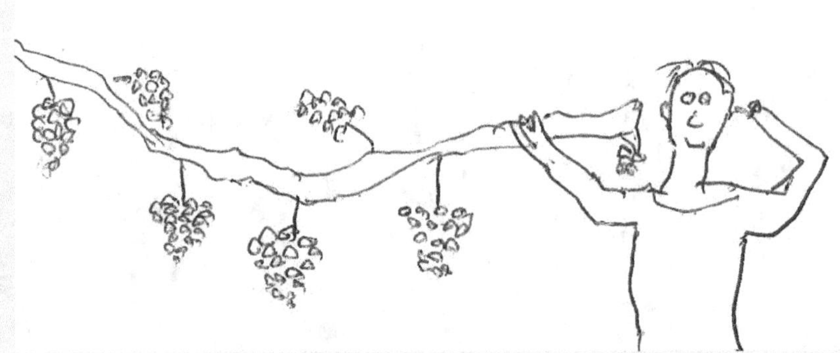

Song 11

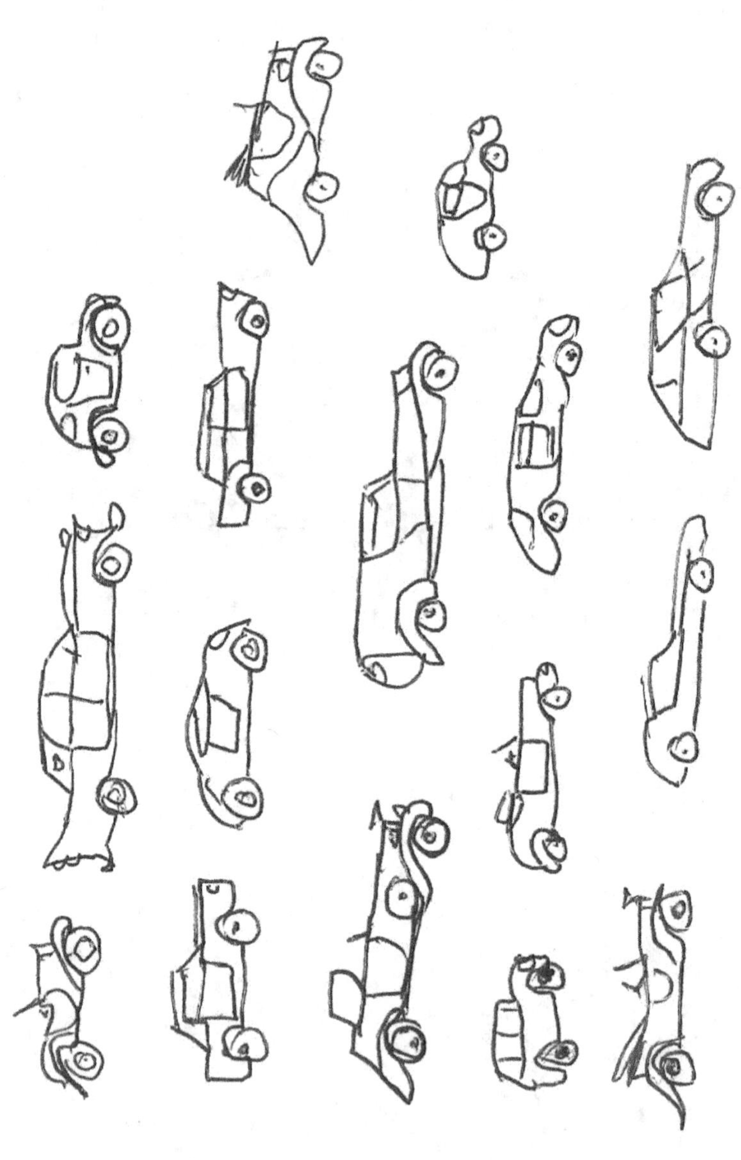

Songs 12 & 13

Song 14

Songs 15 & 16

Song 17

Songs 18 & 19

Song 20

Song 21

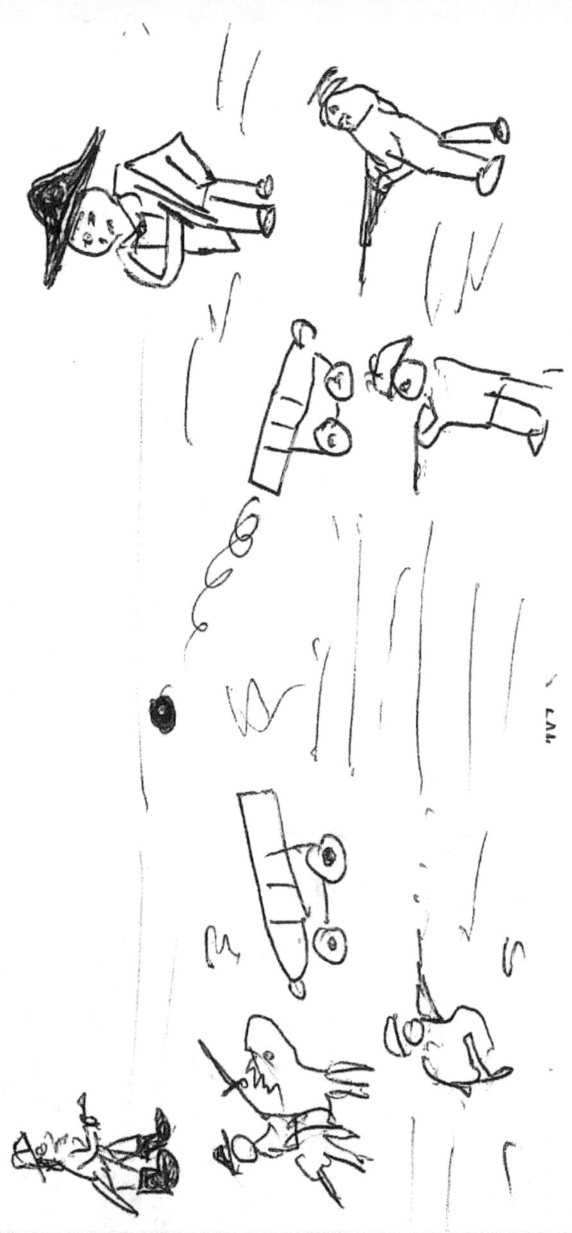

Song 22

Songs 23 & 24

Songs 25 & 26

Song 27

Songs 28 & 29

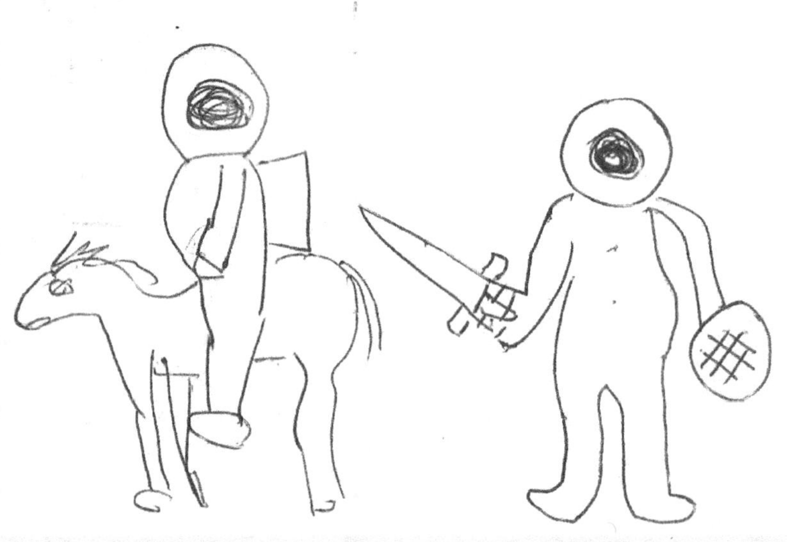

Songs 30 & 31

Songs 32 & 33

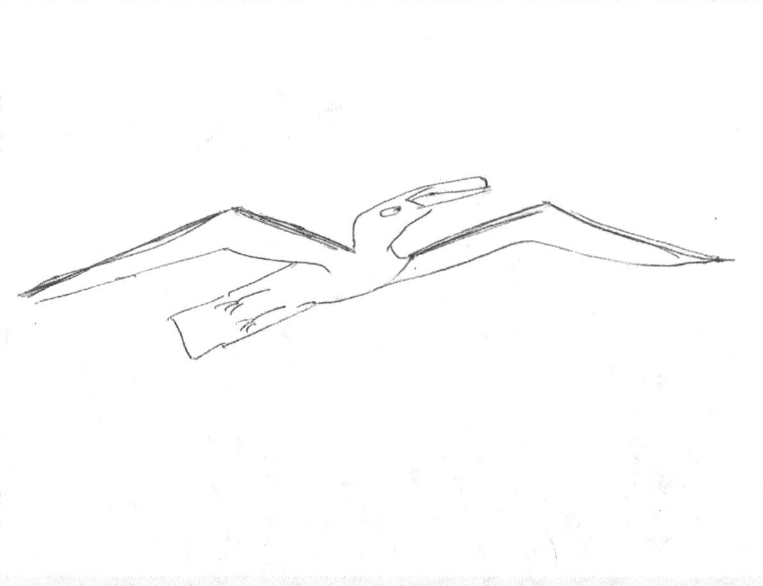

Song 34

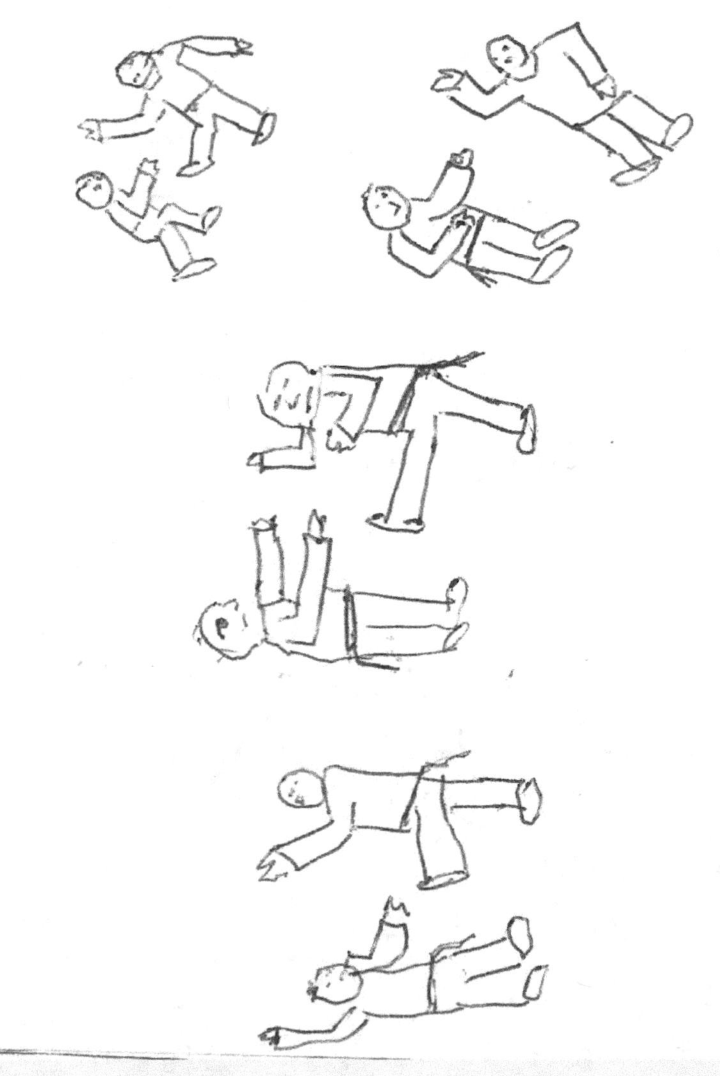

Songs 35 & 36

Song 37

Song 38

Songs 39 & 40

Song 41

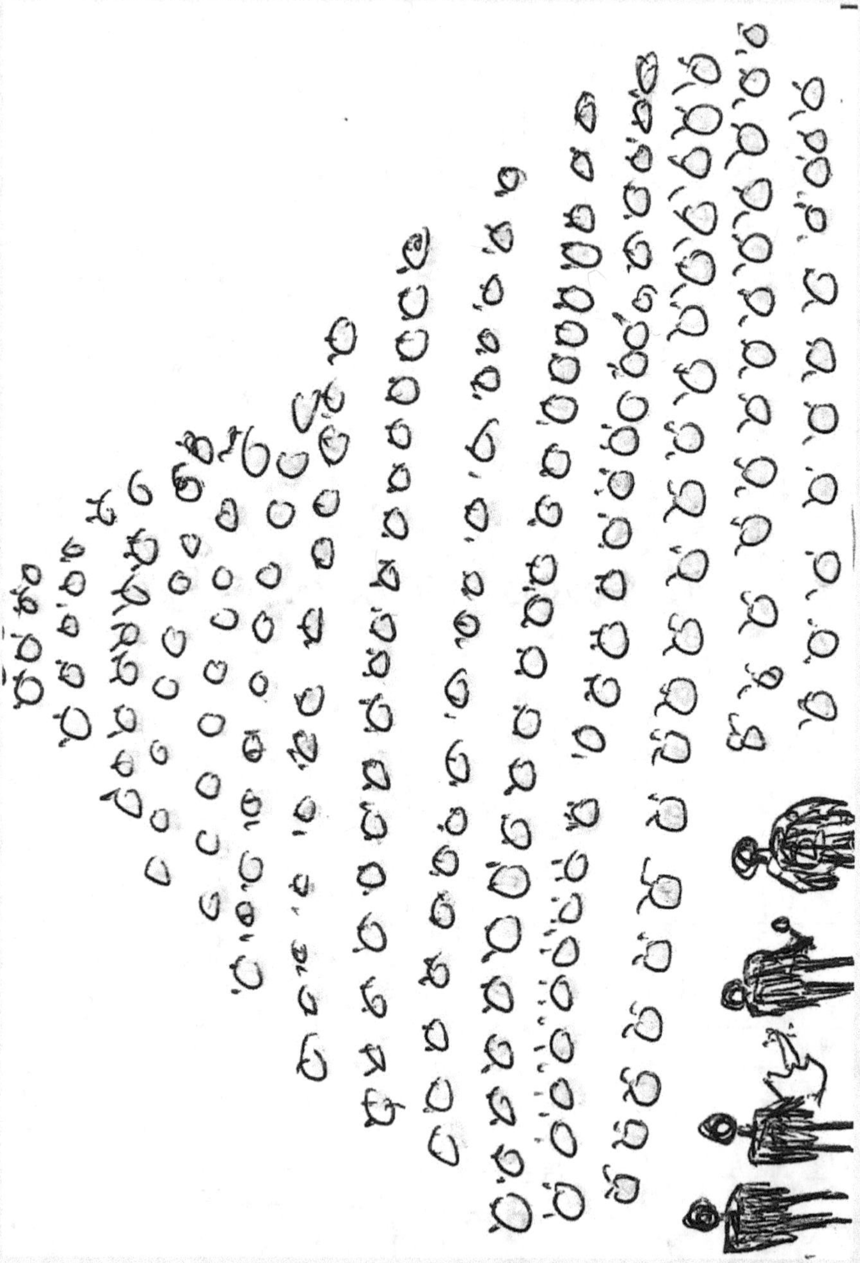

Songs 42 & 43

Songs 44 & 45

Songs 46 & 47

Songs 48 & 49

Song 50

Song 51

Songs 52 & 53

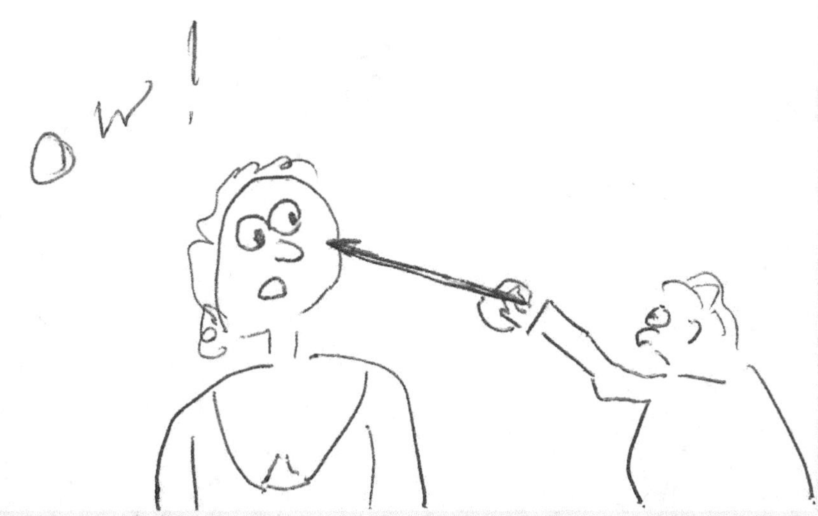

Song 54

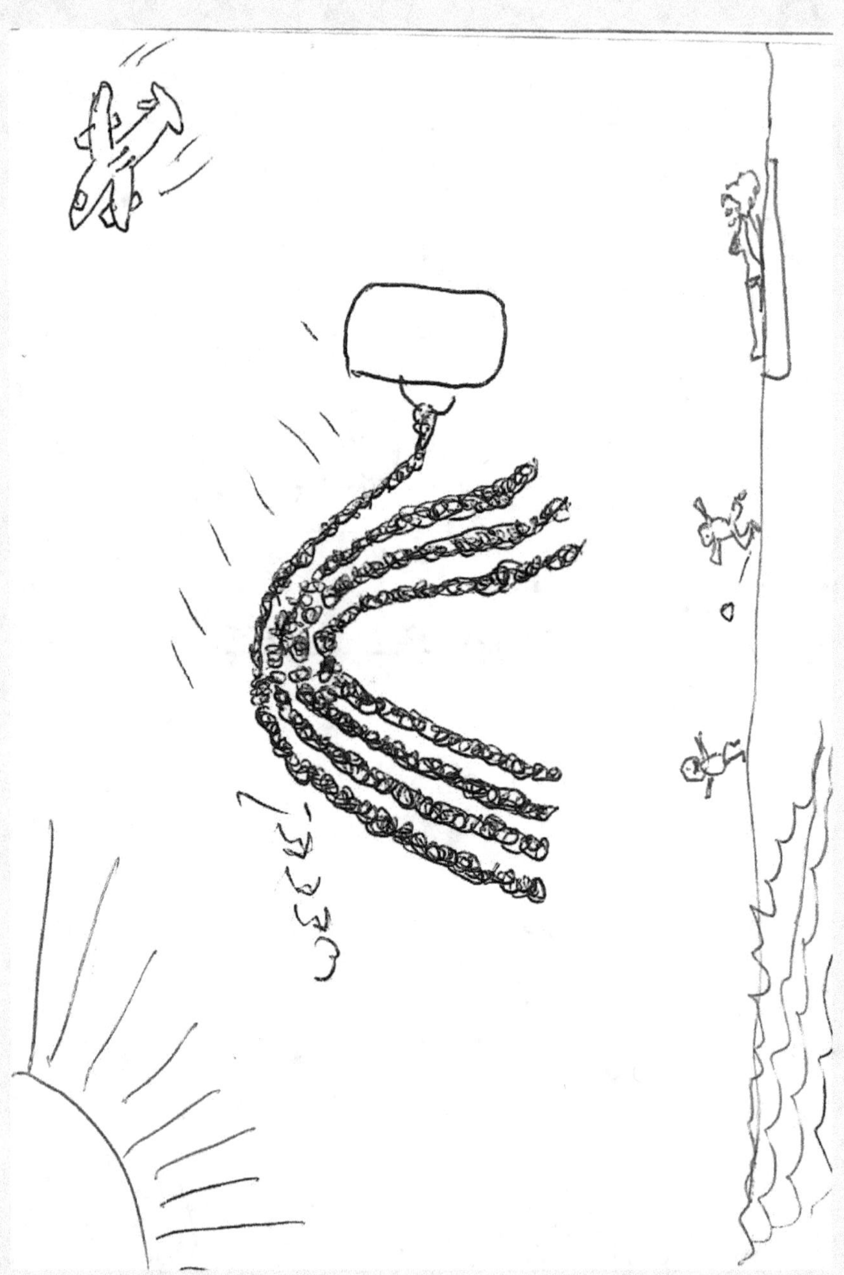

Song 55

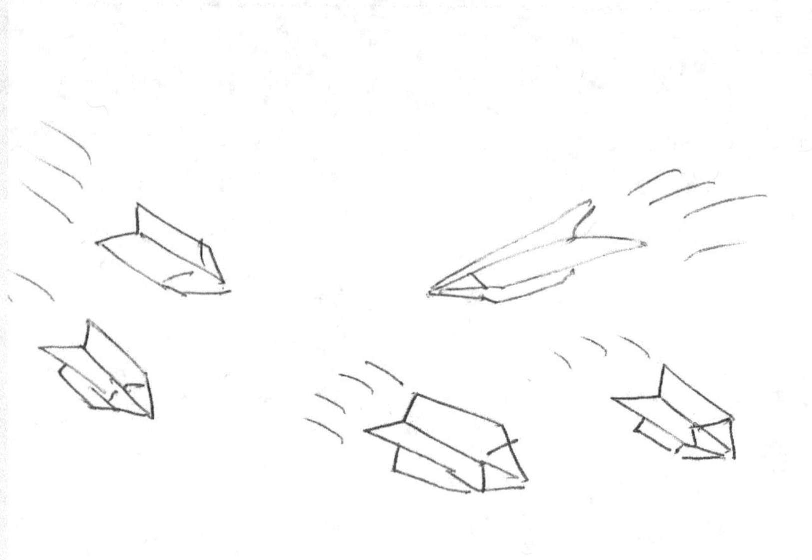

Songs 56 & 57

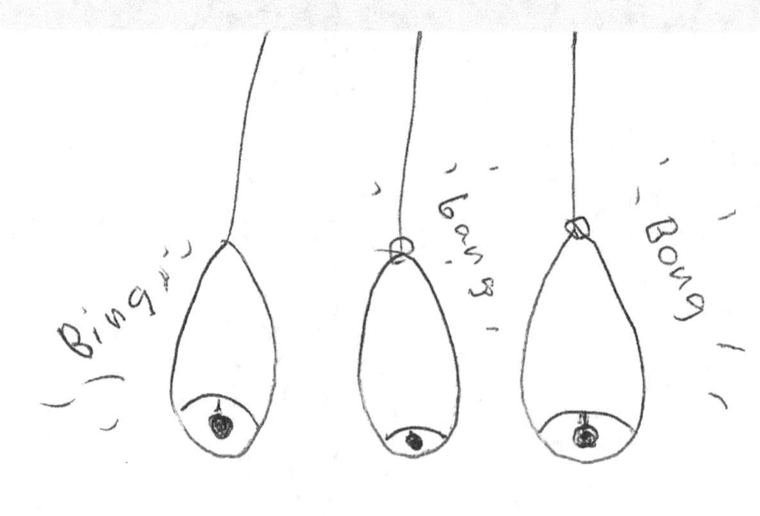

Song 58

Song 59

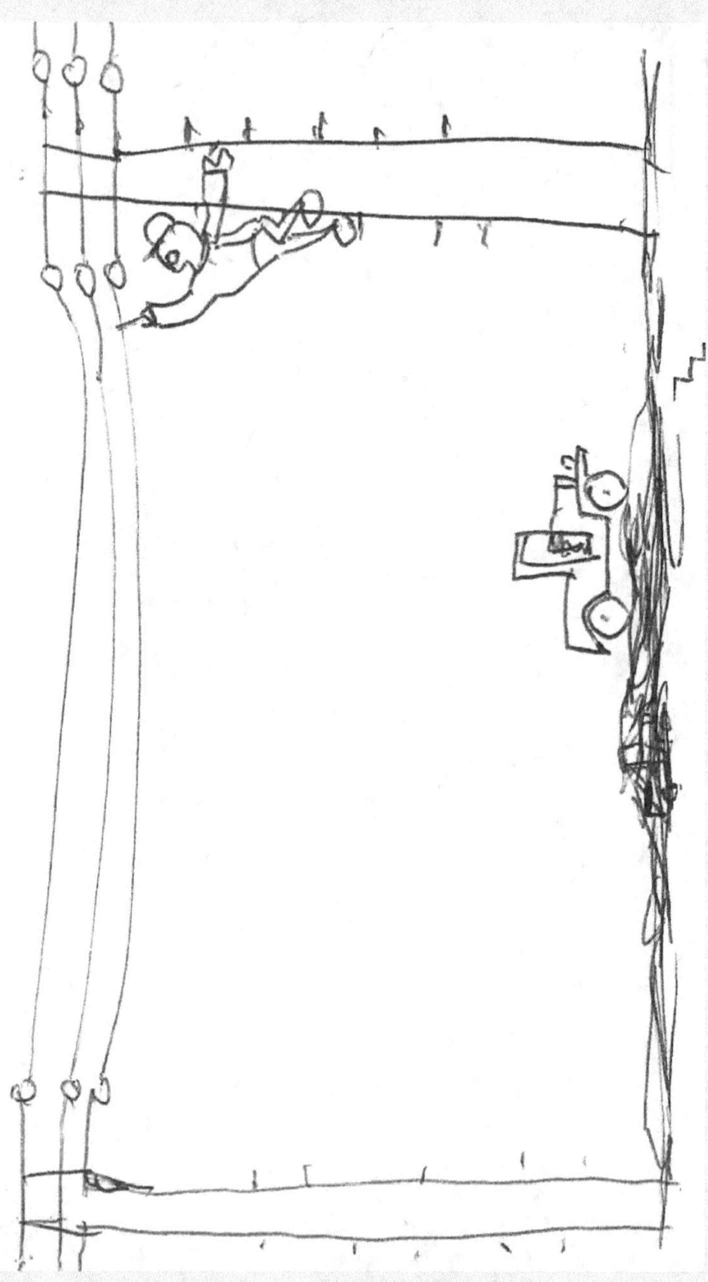

Remembering Gill, one of her favourite songs

Song 60

Songs 61 & 62

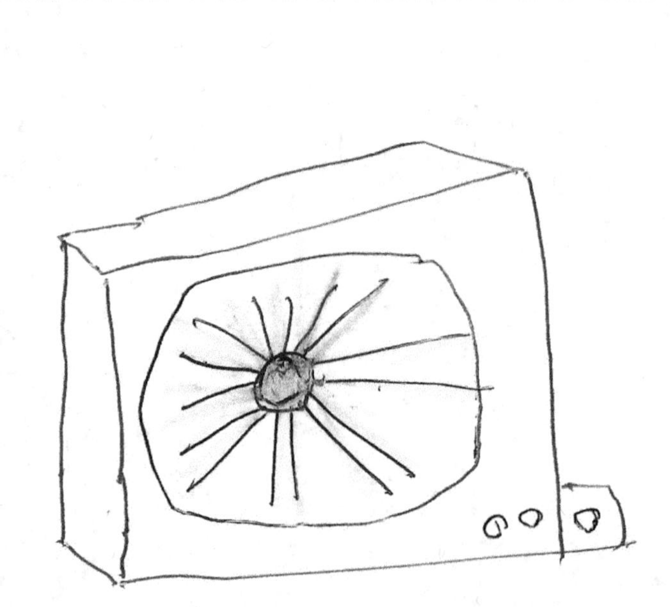

Songs 63 & 64

Song 65

Songs 66 & 67

Love

Song 68

Song 69

Song 70

Song 71

Song 72

Song 73

Wasn't us

Songs 74 & 75

HELLO!

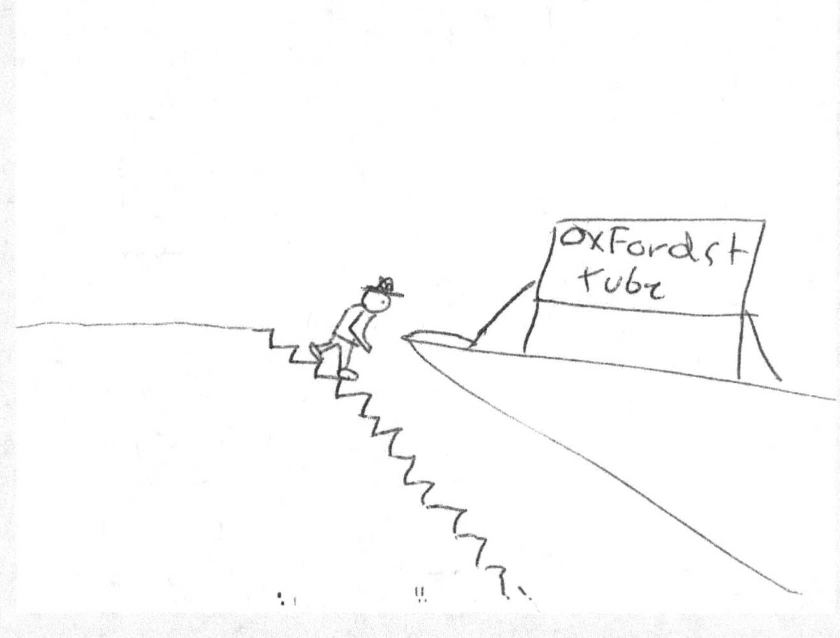

Songs 77 & 78

Song 79

Song 80

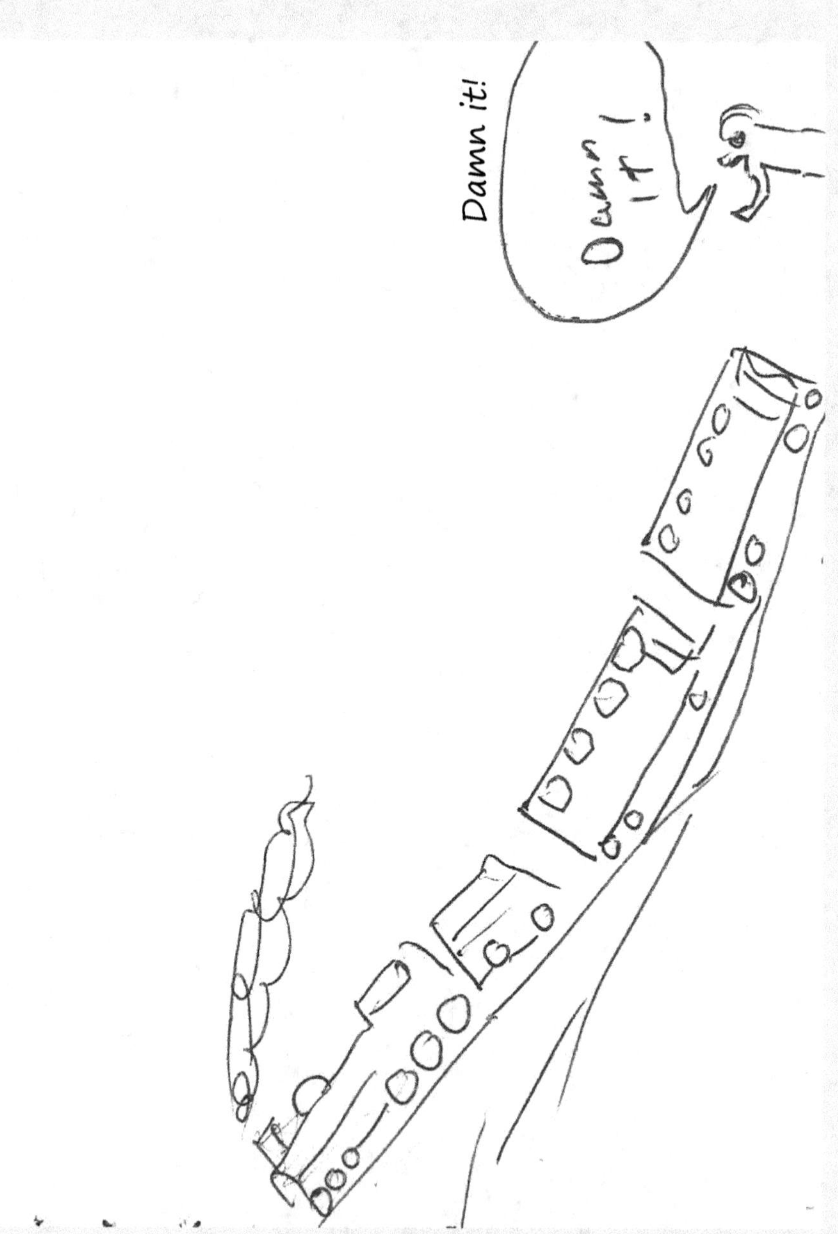

Songs 81 & 82

Songs 83 & 84

Song 85

Did you know smarties were made to make kids smarter
Polo mints, the name was going to be Apollo but NASA sued
m&m's are named after mike and mark the guys who made them first
er... no...

Songs 86 & 87

Say What You See!
Book 1

Available on
Amazon Books

Song List

1. Car Wash, Rose Royce
2. Flowers In the Window, Travis
3. Message In A Bottle, The Police
4. Surfin' U.S.A. The Beach Boys
5. The Boxer, Simon & Garfunkel
6. Paint it, black. Rolling Stones
7. California Dreamin' The Mamas & The Papas
8. Bridge Over Troubled Water, Simon & Garfunkel
9. Mr. Tambourine Man, Bob Dylan
10. I Heard It Through The Grape Vine, Gladys Knight & The Pips
11. Cars, Gary Numan
12. House Of The Rising Sun, The Animals
13. Another Cup Of Coffee, Mike & The Mechanics
14. Fast Car, Tracy Chapman
15. Candle In The Wind, Elton John
16. Get Off Of My Cloud, Rolling Stones

17. Fashion, David Bowie

18. These Boots Are Made For Walkin'
Nancy Sinatra

19. Eye Of The Tiger, Survivor

20. Last Christmas, Wham!

21. Waterloo, ABBA

22. Octopus's Garden, The Beatles

23. Romeo & Juliet, Dire Straits

24. Genie In A Bottle, Christina Aguilera

25. Dancing On The Ceiling, Lionel Richie

26. It's Raining Men, The Weather Girls

27. Man On The Moon, R.E.M

28. When Doves Cry, Prince

29. Umbrella, Rihanna

30. Nights In White Satin, The Moody
Blues

31. Bat Out Of Hell, Meat Loaf

32. Murder On The Dancefloor, Sophie
Ellis-Bextor

33. Albatross, Fleetwood Mac

34. Kung Fu Fighting, Carl Douglas

35. Papa Was A Rollin' Stone,
The Temptations

36. Sledgehammer, Peter Gabriel

37. Ferry Cross The Mersey, Gerry & The
Pacemakers

38. The Combine Harvester, The Wurzels

39. I Shot The Sheriff, Bob Marley & The
Wailers

40. Another Brick In The Wall, Pink Floyd

41. Strawberry Fields Forever, The Beatles

42. Jailhouse Rock, Elvis Presley

43. Killer Queen, Queen

44. Running Up That Hill, Kate Bush

45. Can't Get You Out Of My Head, Kylie
Minogue

46. (Sittin' On) The Dock Of The Bay, Otis
Redding

47. Crazy Horses, The Osmonds

48. Down Under, Men At Work

49. See You Later Alligator, Bill Haley &
Comets

50. God Save The Queen, Sex Pistols

51. The Chain, Fleetwood Mac

52. Hit Me With Your Rhythm Stick, Ian Dury & The Blockheads

53. Poker Face, Lady Gaga

54. Dreadlocks Holiday, 10cc

55. Gypsies, Tramps & Thieves, Cher

56. Paper Planes, M.I.A

57. Tubular Bells, Mike Oldfield

58. Cool For Cats, Squeeze

59. Wichita Lineman, Glen Campbell

60. We Built This City, Starship

61. Big Yellow Taxi, Joni Mitchell

62. The Sun Always Shines On T.V, A-ha

63. Sharp Dressed Man, ZZ Top

64. Papa's Got A Brand New Bag, James Brown

65. A Horse With No Name, America

66. Sk8er Boi, Avril Lavigne

67. Addicted To Love, Robert Palmer

68. Dancing In The Streets, Martha & The Vandellas

69. Don't Stand So Close To Me, The Police

70. Highway To Hell, AC/DC

71. Ghost Town, The Specials

72. Holding Back The Years, Simply Red

73. This Town Ain't Big Enough For The Both Of Us, Sparks

74. We Didn't Start The Fire, Billy Joel

75. Born To Run, Bruce Springsteen

76. London Calling, The Clash

77. Going Underground, The Jam

78. I Walk The Line, Johnny Cash & The Tennessee Two

79. The Man Who Sold The World, David Bowie

80. Last Train To Clarksville, The Monkeys

81. Video Killed The Radio Star, The Buggles

82. All Along The Watchtower, Jimi Hendrix

83. Flowers In Your Hair, The
Lumineers

84. Tusk, Fleetwood Mac

85. Little Lies, Fleetwood Mac

86. The Man With The Child In His
Eyes, Kate Bush

87. Whisky In A Jar, Thin Lizzy

Sample pages from
Name That Town!

Towns 57 & 58

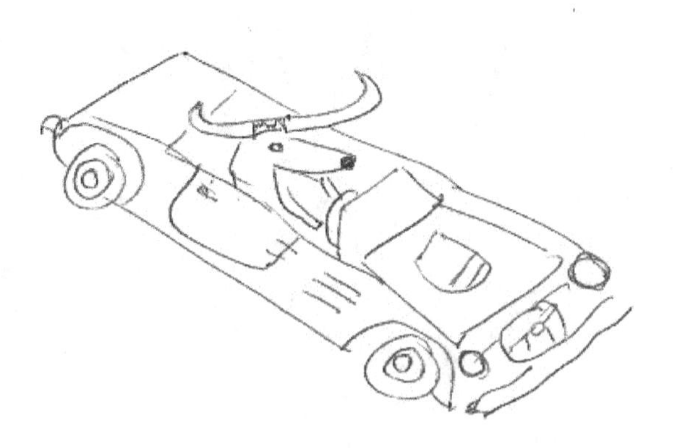

Towns 7 & 8

Name That Film!

Expected release date February 2025

www.ingramcontent.com/pod-product-compliance
Lightning Source LLC
Chambersburg PA
CBHW061308250726
48653CB00002B/840